# Blacks, Indians & Women
## in America's
## War for Independence

## DUDLEY C
# GOULD

D1264198

**Southfarm Press,** *Publisher*
www.war-books.com
**Middletown, Connecticut**

ISBN-10: 0-913337-57-9
ISBN-13: 978-0-913337-57-8

Most of this work was previously published as
part of *Times of Brother Jonathan* by Dudley C Gould;
copyright © 2001 by Dudley C Gould
and published by Southfarm Press.

Every effort has been made to locate the copyright holders
of all copyrighted materials and to secure the necessary
permission to reproduce them. In the event of any questions
arising as to their use, the publisher will make
necessary changes in future printings.
**Attention: Educational Institutions**
Southfarm Press books are available at quantity discounts
with bulk purchase for educational use. For information,
please write to Special Sales Department
at our address shown above.

**Visit our Web Site at http://www.war-books.com**

# *Contents*

# Introduction

Early American historians, solely responsible for discovering and disclosing past events to the public, avoided mentioning women as they did Blacks and Jews and any other controversial or 'unimportant' subject. After reading about the American Revolutionary War as reported by 18th century New England historians and their imitators, one is left with the impression there were no Black warriors, Indians or noteworthy women on the combat scene. The following pages tell a different story.

# 1

# *Blacks*

King George's sycophant, Dr. Samuel Johnson, typified British reaction to the American clamor for freedom—

> *Let us give the Indians arms, teach them disci-*
> *pline, and encourage them now and then to*
> *plunder a plantation. Why do we hear the loud-*
> *est yelps for liberty from the drivers of Negroes.*

British historian Sir George Trevelyan, throughout his four-volume history of the War of Independence, was generally in sympathy with the American cause, but on the issue of slavery took angry exception—

> *Their American sense of humor was already*
> *sufficiently developed for them to perceive that*

*allusions to Negroes should be sparingly intro-*
*duced into a document which proclaimed it a*
*self-evident truth that men are equal, and en-*
*dorsed by their creator with unalienable right to*
*liberty and the pursuit of happiness.*

The moment the call went out for civilians to become soldiers, April 20, 1775, black men presented themselves. Some were slaves with written permission from
their owners. The Massachusetts Committee of Safety
determined this offer in a curious way as it differentiated
between freemen and slaves, or servants, as the some
5,000 slaves were commonly referred to in New England.
Although no decision was made at the time, they allowed
free Negroes to serve in the American camp at Cambridge, as they were conspicuous on Breed's Hill in June.

One man, Salem Poor, "behaved like an experi-
enced officer as well as an excellent soldier," according to
Colonel William Prescott, who allowed that "they were
obedient soldiers and useful laborers, of a less mutinous
spirit than some of their white brothers."

In the Provincial Continental Congress at Philadelphia, it was voted to bar blacks from the Continental
Army. That was seconded by a council of general officers
before John Murrow, Fourth Lord of Dunmore, Virginia's
loyal governor. The proclamation was made in November 1775, freeing all black indentured servants, black
birds, slaves who were able and willing to bear arms for
the king to join the British Army.

Washington in turn issued an order allowing
Continental recruiting officers to enlist free blacks,
bringing the matter of color to the attention of Congress,

which, without debate, permitted those who had served faithfully and well at Lexington, Cambridge, and Breed's Hill to reenlist.

Blacks continued to serve in the Continental Army despite all legislative efforts of southern representatives to exclude them. Black soldiers met with approval in most provinces. Their record at Breed's Hill spread widely by word of mouth. Rhode Island, the first to profess freedom of religion to all, bought up slaves who volunteered to fight for everyone's liberty and enrolled them as soldiers, many going to the all-black regiment of Colonel Christopher Greene. A return in Washington's immediate command, the Main Army, showed that several brigades each had an average of 54 blacks, and one German officer noted in 1777—

> One sees no regiment in which there are not
> Negroes in abundance, and among them are
> able-bodied, sturdy fellows.

Hessian regimental commander, Major General Donlop (killed at Princeton) bought a 13-year-old black boy, taught him German and bequeathed him to the Minister of the State of Hesse-Kassel. Baron von Riedesal took home a volunteer black drum corps, recruited in part to fill out an infantry battalion. Lieutenant General de Rochambeau and other French officers purchased slaves at Rhode Island and paid black freemen to be military servants. Rebel Dan Morgan liberated two young boys from the British at Cowpens to slave for him the rest of his life. Upon his death, Nat and Tony were freed and given small legacies.

In 1775, Sam Adams and John Hancock, part of the second Massachusetts delegation to the Continental Congress, left Boston in Hancock's lavish coach and four. Two armed white servants were up front and four black servants (slaves) behind, two on horseback and two riding as footmen to push the carriage out of mud holes and perform other such tasks.

General Washington kept several slaves with him as he trouped the battlefields fighting for the freedom of whites. The General bought his favorite, Billy Lee, in 1768 for £61. A sound male slave in 1772 on the block at Botetourt County, Virginia, with no special abilities, cost £8, £1 more than a horse and £3 less than a rifle. One of the other five slaves in the General's military retinue, Hannah, was bought from a minister of the gospel.

The Church of England in America owned slaves and accepted them as a form of endowment. When the Reverend Cotton Mather of Boston was presented with a black slave girl by his congregation, he recorded the event in his diary as "a smile from heaven." He lectured Boston slaves in a sermon, *Fondness for Freedom*, on May 21, 1721, "many of you live comfortably in very easy servitude and should give thanks that God was so easy."

The year he died, Washington, who owed an immeasurable debt to his loyal black soldiers, especially toward the end of the war when so few whites answered the call, wrote to brother-in-law George Lewis —

> *The running off of my cook has been a most inconvenient thing to the family and what rendered it more disagreeable is that I resolved never to become the master of another slave by*

*purchase, but this resolution I fear I must break.*
*I have endeavored to hire black or white but I am*
*not yet supplied.*

The cook's name was Hercules.

Those who would not be conscience-stricken were suddenly panic-stricken when rumor spread throughout the South that slaves who murdered their masters would be given their estates. This threat became an even more compelling reason for slaveholders, north and south, to fear those whose freedom they denied while actively seeking their own, as the potential military services of up to 600,000 blacks were declared "intestine enemies" by southern governors.

The *New York Journal* greeted Lord Dunmore on its front page —

*Hail! Doughty Ethiopian chief!*
*Thou ignominious Negro thief!*
*These blacks shall prop thy sinking name,*
*And damn thee to perpetual fame.*

Dunmore was able to collect almost a thousand blacks, giving them emblems to wear on their chests that stated, "Liberty to Slaves," the way organizations today hand out printed T-shirts. The only engagement of this British all-black unit was a defeat at Big Bridge near Norfolk.

His plan failed otherwise for two reasons, a small-pox epidemic swept through their quarters aboard British ships in the harbor and the grapevine informed them of greedy British brass, who after several plundering raids in the guise of freeing and enlisting slaves, gathered 2,000 and sold them to English planters in the Sugar Islands. Chief Engineer Major James Moncrief alone shipped 800 slaves from Charleston to the West Indies as personal property. In fact, many escapees and liberated slaves found that they were merely trading chains. Former slaves who were captured fighting for the British were not considered prisoners of war or freemen by southern forces. They were turned over to civilian authorities to be handled as runaways.

Finally, distrustful of all whites, one band of 300 slaves refused to board ships in Georgia with the evacuating British even though they continued to proudly style themselves King of England soldiers. They escaped to exist in swamps near Savannah, pillaging until captured by militia in 1786.

Jefferson estimated that some 30,000 slaves from Virginia alone escaped during the war, supposedly to freedom, but, exposed to white man's diseases more so than when living healthy lives in the fields, all but 3,000 who sought safety with the British died behind British lines. Only one-eighth of the slaves held before the war were made to go with their Loyalist owners when they left the States at the war's end.

At the parley ending the war, the United States Minister was instructed to demand compensation for lost slaves, which the British refused even to consider because they had never officially recognized slavery. Jefferson was as disappointed as anyone, having lost 30 of his 83 slaves to Tarleton's raiders.

A letter from attorney James McHenry, former aide to General Washington and one day Secretary of

War, asked his help in recovering "Negro man Jacob in your army," owned by McHenry's client, Mary Gulany, "one of the best old ladies in the world." The letter was typical and so was Washington's reply. If Jacob could be found, he would be more valuable toiling in the army. In fact, Jacob could easily have been found risking his life "in his Marquis's department."

When the Marquis de Lafayette made a return visit to the United States in 1824, he was reunited in Richmond with that loyal old soldier, a black man who called himself Jacob Lafayette. Jacob was just one of many who volunteered to bear responsibility of citizenship before being in a position to enjoy its rights.

British Army orderly books are still scattered with such picturesque names of enlistees in America as Liberty, Freedom, John Francisco, Simon Congo, Anthony Portuguese, Negro Lew, or whatever single name the enlistee gave. When in either a British or an American orderly book, a black was unable to give a proper name recognizable to the recruiter, "a Negro man" was written beside his witnessed X; presumably he would find a name before re-enlisting.

The French recruited 545 blacks from Santo Domingo (including what is now Haiti), and there were 700 black soldiers in Fontage's Legion alone, free men and slaves designated Volunteer Chasseurs, to serve under General Marquis de Saint-Simon at the disastrous battle of Savannah in 1779. There, more blacks fell than in all the rest of the war. Among this force was a 13-year-old servant named Henri Christophe, later the tyrant king of Haiti.

The name Claude Henri de Rouvroy, Comte de

Saint-Simon, is engraved on a granite obelisk outside the Kremlin walls in Moscow, one line below Marx and Lenin, for his contribution to what was to evolve by degrees into socialism and then rapidly degenerate into militant, dictatorial communism. It is ironic that Claude, a pioneer socialist, contributed as he did to the birth of the modern world's first capitalistic state.

Combat knowledge and military self-reliance acquired by Haitian blacks at Savannah, along with malaria and yellow fever, enabled sons and grandsons of those blacks who survived a Haitian uprising in 1803 to be the first in the world to defeat Napoleon Bonaparte. The defeat ensured that the French, unable to fulfill military plans for an empire west of the Mississippi, would, in 1803, be willing to sell the Louisiana Territory.

As late as 1781, Colonel Thomas Sumter, of South Carolina, was offering black slaves as a bonus for reenlisting: One adult black for a private white soldier, and three grown slaves and one small one for a colonel's reenlistment. He was dealing in slave futures, planning to capture the blacks after he enlisted enough whites with his barbaric recruiting promise. Beginning the year before, Virginia voted to do the same, to give every white male recruit who enlisted for the duration of the war 300 acres of land, plus a healthy black between the ages of 20 and 30, or £60 in gold or silver.

The Baron du Bourg, professional soldier, wrote —

*I cannot insist too strongly how surprised I was by the American Army. It is truly incredible that troops almost naked, poorly paid and composed of old men, children and negroes should behave so well on the march and under fire.*

Few if any blacks today attend exclusive functions of the Daughters or Sons of the American Revolution, and black singer Marian Anderson was even forbidden in 1939 to appear at the DAR Constitution Hall, yet few descendants of those who fought the War of Independence are more deserving.

The U. S. Army can brag that it was the first to respond to President Harry Truman's Executive Order in 1948 to integrate, even as it had been integrated in the heat of battle from sheer necessity during the War of Independence and every war since. No white serves with more justifiable pride in the U.S. Armed Forces with a longer, more heroic heritage, earned against such great odds. Only very recently has the white world been told how well and in what numbers blacks served in our freedom fight, that is, freedom for whites.

An estimated 8,000 blacks, free and enslaved, fought in the rebel infantry during the eight years of war, which, considering their background of misery, is remarkable. The Adjutant General's return on just one day, August 24, 1778, disclosed 755 blacks on active duty, not counting many hundred hangers-on and laborers not enlisted. A fact seldom mentioned by white historians, and never until the mid-1960s and the advent of national civil rights. Those blacks were, however, recognized by most foreign observers, as the French officer Ludwig Baron de Clausen, who wrote in July 1781 from the rebel camp at White Plains, New York —

*I had a chance to see the American Army, man for*

[13]

*man. It is really painful to see these brave men, almost naked with only some trousers and little linen jackets, most of them without stockings, but, would you believe it, very cheerful and healthy in appearance. A quarter of them are Negroes, merry, confident and sturdy. It is incredible that soldiers composed of men of every age, even children of fifteen, of whites and blacks, unpaid and rather poorly fed, can march so fast and withstand fire so steadfastedly.*

English-speaking Clausen came to America as a subaltern in the Royal Deux-Ponts Regiment and soon became a valued member of Rochambeau's staff, especially in liaison work with Americans.

Pennsylvania Major Persifor Frazer described a battalion of New Englanders "among whom is the strangest mixtures of Negroes and Indians and whites, with old men and young children." And Brigadier General John Thomas, hero of two American wars—

*In the regiments at Roxbury we had some Negroes. I look on them in general as equal in serviceability with other men for fatigue and in action; many of them have proved themselves brave.*

Private Jesse Likens of Thompson's Pennsylvania riflemen wrote home from Cambridge about "such Negroes, such colonels, such boys and such grand-fathers" and there were so many blacks among the volunteers around Cambridge that General Artemis Ward ordered adjutants of the grand Army to "note the complexion of the soldiers" in their morning reports. During the combat hysteria of the British rout from Concord, based on the sightings of many black volunteers, some armed only with pitchforks, it was rumored that the long-dreaded slave uprising was taking place.

Rhode Island's First Regiment mustered with 175 blacks, only 30 of whom were free men. Although not commonly known, there were plantations and breweries in Rhode Island, Massachusetts, and Connecticut worked by many hundreds of slaves. Ten percent of Newport, Rhode Island, was black, and black slaves built the Jewish synagogue there.

Early in 1778, the colony provided for the voluntary enrollment of slaves, brave adventuresome young men willing to die for freedom. Those who stepped forward, if lucky enough to survive the fighting and deadly camp diseases, would be emancipated. The state made a partial compensation to each slave's former master who, incidentally, drew the black soldier's pay while he fought.

As the tiresome war dragged on, the 1st Rhode Island Infantry became virtually all black and was cited by Congress for exceptional bravery at Butt's Hill in the tricky retreat from Newport. Colonel Christopher Greene, first cousin of General Nathanael Greene, commanded the regiment. He was killed in a minor scuffle at Westchester, New York, toward the end of the war. Wrote de Clausen —

*Three-quarters of the Rhode Island regiment consists of Negroes. It is the most neatly dressed, the best under arms and the most precise in its movements.*

[15]

Christopher's men influenced cousin Nat's opinion —

> *There's a spirit of enterprising among the black*
> *people; and those that come out as volunteers*
> *are not a little formidable to the enemy.*

The British knew who they fought and documented it with several stanzas to "Yankee Doodle" —

> *The rebel clowns, oh what sight!*
> *Too awkward was their figure;*
> *'Twas yonder stood a pious wight*
> *And here and there a nigger.*

And after the defeat at Yorktown, the Americans —

> *The women ran, the darkies too,*
> *And all the bells they tolled;*
> *For Britain's sons, by Doodle doo,*
> *We're sure to be consoled.*

One foreigner, Polish engineer Colonel Tadeusz Andrei Bonadvantura Kosciuszko, was so impressed by the blacks' bravery and plight he left $14,000 in his will "to establish a school for free blacks," which his relatives in Poland successfully contested. General John Patterson gave Brother Thad a black slave named Grippy who claimed to be the son of a prince, and who could honestly refute him? Kosciuszko tried to take Grippy to Poland as his paid body servant but Grippy, who distrusted both sides, went AWOL in New York on the eve of embarkation and returned to Patterson who, touched by his action, immediately set him free. Grippy bought a small farm at Stockbridge, Massachusetts, where he rounded out his days quietly as a beloved and highly respected prince of royal African blood.

Because blacks had never been tested in America as a unit, and no American had direct knowledge of their former lives, there could be no valid opinion of the fighting ability and courage of black warriors, so they were compared only by the unfortunate inferior station in white man's society.

There were those, of course, who knew the truth, and in May 1799, South Carolinian John Laurens raised a regiment of blacks to lift the siege of Charleston. There, armed slaves were killed or captured fighting beside their rebel masters. Most white survivors were paroled and exchanged, but the British sold the black Rebels into a far worse slavery in the hopeless cane fields of the West Indies.

Laurens wrote to Washington —

*Had we arms for three thousand such black men as I could select in Carolina, I should have no doubt of success in driving the British out of Georgia, and subduing East Florida before the end of July.*

and to his father —

*I would advance those who are unjustly deprived of the rights of mankind to state which would be a proper gradation between abject slavery and perfect liberty.... I am tempted to believe that this*

[17]

*trampled people have so much human left in them as to be capable of aspiring to the rights of men by noble exertions, if some friend of mankind would point the road, and give them a prospect of success.... Habits of subordination, patience under fatigues, sufferings and deprivations of every kind, are soldierly qualifications, which these men possess in an eminent degree*

George Washington noted that it was the institution of slavery, not the character of slaves, that placed obstacles in the way and he replied cautiously —

*The policy of arming slaves is in my opinion a moot point unless the enemy set the example. For, should we begin to form battalions of them I have not the smallest doubt, if the war is to be prosecuted, of their following us in it and justifying the measure upon our own ground. The contest must then be, who can arm fastest, and where are our arms?*

The General's cautious reply to Laurens is a bit puzzling but not impossible to understand coming from a slave holder, since at the time he was wrong to say "their following us in it."

He seems to have changed his mind, for before that in his general order at Valley Forge on February 2, 1778, Washington was usually sympathetic —

*A well chosen body of five thousand black men, properly officered to act as a light infantry, in ad-*

*dition to our present establishment, might give us a decisive success in the next campaign. We have long deplored the wretched state of these men.... The bloody wars in Africa to furnish America with these slaves, the groans of the despairing multitudes toiling for the luxuries of merciless tyrants. His excellency is convinced that the numerous tribes of blacks in the southern parts of the Continent offer a resource to us that should not be neglected.*

The threat and reality of Dunmore's Ethiopians had already been made, the precedent of using blacks established. As for the value of black soldiers when properly motivated, this was well known to Washington also via the exploits of the Virginia frontiersman Captain Jack, alias the Black Hunter, known and feared by Indians as the Black Rifle.

After returning one day to find his wife and children scalped, their bodies mutilated, Captain Jack turned to a lifetime of rage, killing Indians for pleasure. He and a band of equally savage backwoods renegades, many crazed for the same reason as Captain Jack, were called The Long Hunters for their customs of ranging many miles beyond the frontier into trackless wildernesses butchering Indians. Had Braddock accepted their assistance, no matter how undisciplined they were, his army would never have fallen into the trap it did.

Young Laurens was of French Huguenot extraction. His father was a slave merchant until 1762, when he became aggressively against slavery. Laurens was educated in Switzerland and was sociologically well ahead of his unrefined fellow Americans. He was the only American to request and receive an audience with Louis XVI, in 1780, and also to have the king order immediate aid to the Continental Congress. Unfortunately, Laurens was killed in the last battle of the war on James Island near Charleston. Soldiers of both races knew they had lost a good friend. His last words —

> *I would cherish those dear ragged Continentals whose patience will be the admiration of future ages and I glory in bleeding with them.*

West Indian native Alexander Hamilton recommended to Congress —

> *Negroes will make very excellent soldiers. This project will have to combat prejudice and self-interest. Contempt for the blacks makes us fancy many things that are not founded in reason or experience. Their natural faculties are as good as ours. Give them their freedom with their muskets; it will secure their fidelity, animate their courage and have a good influence upon those who remain, by opening the door to their emancipation.*

Those in Congress who forbade the enlistment of blacks or Indians included Edward Rutledge of South Carolina, who moved that blacks already enlisted be kicked out. His proposal was dismissed summarily and on January 16, 1776, with the war but a year old, so few whites were enlisting or re-enlisting that the Congressional ban was lifted to allow blacks and Indians to join the Continental Line.

To fill quotas in Continental units, many New England township committees presented black slaves as substitutes for drafted whites. Both Barrington and Durham, New Hampshire, at one time signed up five black slaves each. Plymouth, Massachusetts, signed up six at another time for three-year hitches in the regulars, if they lasted that long, allowing the same number of Puritans to stay home and pray.

By 1779, not only did Congress *allow* blacks, they compensated slave owners a sum "not to exceed a thousand dollars for each able-bodied black slave of standard size, not exceeding thirty-five years of age." The slaves received no enlistment bonus or pay as did whites, "but be clothed and fed by government." If a slave served well and faithfully and survived the war, he was to be set free and handed $50 with which to start a new life. True to form, Congress reneged on separation money and land, but did give certificates of emancipation.

Rutledge also complained that dividing prizes, as was customary among privateers and the British Navy, "would make sailors selfish, piratical, mercenary, bent wholly on plunder." Adams went along with this and when the suggestion was put into effect, recruitment for the Army's navy ceased. Rutledge's brother John, governor of South Carolina, was equally off base, parleying with British General Augustine Provost to have the state declared neutral and its fate decided at the peace table.

Such traitorous dealing was not uncommon. In November 1775, the good citizens of Bristol, Rhode Island, bribed British Navy Captain Wallace with 40 sheep not to burn the town. General Washington's caretaker,

[21]

cousin Lund Washington, bargained with the captain of the British sloop *Savage* by giving all the food the crew could manage to get aboard in return for not sacking Mount Vernon.

When the General learned of this, he was furious. Promised freedom, 17 of his slaves left voluntarily with the *Savage*. Washington re-enslaved two of them, both young women, at Yorktown, where they had been slaving for the British.

For a time, Connecticut had a full regiment of blacks in General Samuel Holden Parson's brigade, while 750 were enlisted in Maryland in 1781. Colonel Rignier's regiment of New York Continentals were nearly all black and wore wool caps. Many were stranded West Indians who spoke French.

Many blacks fought for the king, not as armed uniformed soldiers, but in menial but essential tasks that relieved British soldiers to fight. Both sides shied away from arming blacks and instead found various laboring and housekeeping jobs for them. It has been estimated that there were some 30,000 slaves and free black men serving in one capacity or another in the British Army during the war, which could hardly have operated with the successes it did in South Carolina and southern North Carolina without black spies and guides. American units were encircled or surprised on a number of occasions, thanks to local freed slaves.

Drummer boys of British regiments were often black, and it was their duty to apply lashes to court-martialed white soldiers, stripped to the waist, tied to crossed sergeant major halberds. John Adams tells how the sight of a white man being whipped by blacks during

Boston's pre-war occupation infuriated Bostonians.

The New York fortification unit, the Black Panthers, were Loyalists and the Hessian Erb Prinz Regiment, for one, hired blacks to replace casualties. To one black Loyalist goes the credit of having one of the most miraculous escapes of all time. Freeman Benjamin Whitcoff, British undercover agent from Long Island, having spied for two years, was finally caught in New Jersey and hanged. After swinging three minutes, he was cut down and revived by a raiding party of British dragoons. Whitcoff's father fought for the Rebels.

Service by blacks, when noticed at all in the writings of white Americans, was usually reported in a derogatory manner, as when Washington wrote to the president of Congress from his Cambridge headquarters, "From the number of boys, deserters and Negroes which have been enlisted in this province, I entertain some doubts whether the number required can be raised at all."

Sounds like the complaint made by Admiral Oliver Perry in 1813, at a low ebb of the War of 1812, "Congress has given me nothing but soldiers, blacks and cripples." With them, he won the battle of Lake Erie, one of the most decisive of that war.

In the autumn of 1777, General Philip Schuyler of Albany, New York, complained that a third of his force were "Negroes, boys and men too aged for field or, indeed, any service. Negroes are a disgrace to our arms. It is inconsistent with the Sons of Freedom to trust their all to be defended by slaves." How could Schuyler know? His own military failings were investigated by Congress. Schuyler never led anyone in combat, and he resigned in the middle of the war to resume his money-making career.

While Colonel Benedict Arnold and his men suffered extremely in the northern wilderness and while Ethan Allen was making a quixotic assault on Montreal, aristocrat Major General Schuyler lost Canada. Schuyler procrastinated, retreated without orders, made many unnerving indecisions, suffered convenient illnesses and showed a total lack of leadership. By the time he relinquished command to General Richard Montgomery, all attack momentum was gone and morale was at a consistent low. Troops in such a spoiled mode should have been pulled off the line, resupplied, and regrouped.

A black slave, Prince Estabrook of Captain Jonas Parker's company who fought at Lexington, was said to have been the son of an African chief, as were several outstandingly brave blacks.

A number of blacks, free and enslaved, fought alongside whites on Breed's Hill without the benefit of militia training. The names of but a few are recorded in one diary or another, as Cato Stedman and Cato Boardman, and Nero Benson, who went about tooting on a banged-up trumpet he found, when he wasn't pulling the trigger of a fallen-man's musket. Another heroic soldier-slave, Caesar Bascom, died in a pool of his dark red blood atop Breed's Hill, exhorting his white maties to "give them one for old Caesar."

Salem Poor's bravery on Breed's Hill warranted a petition on his behalf to Congress signed by 14 Massachusetts officers who witnessed his steadfast position, loading and firing a musket, even as men to his sides gave way. Poor never received a thank you or any further recognition, although he went on to fight at White Plains and to suffer at Valley Forge.

Slave Pompey Blackman, owned by Joshua Boylston, fought at Lexington and Breed's Hill before being submitted as a substitute for a white and serving out the war in the Continental Line. And there were Cuff Whittemore and Caleb How of Plymouth and Titus Colburn, Alexander Ames and Basilar Lew of Andover. Cato Freeman of Andover wasn't himself a free man, however, until he put in three years in the Continentals, until he was free of the British and, at last, of whites altogether.

From Peterbourgh, New Hampshire, were Samuel Wefs and Titus Wilson. And there were at least two black citizen soldiers at Trenton, known and remembered by diarists for years to come, Oliver Cromwell and Prince Whipple. Prince, the war-freed slave of Captain William Whipple of Portsmouth, New Hampshire, helped row Washington across the Delaware, which made him a lifelong celebrity back home.

Peter Salem, slave of the Belknaps, in Captain Simon Edgleis's company of Massachusetts militia, was crippled for life by a British ball in his left shoulder. He was famous throughout New England for picking off Major John Pitcairn of the Royal Marines. Ex-slave, badly wounded, Prince Estabrook was remembered years after that fateful day by Captain Frederick Macknezi, adjutant of the Royal Welch Fusiliers.

Salem was freed on the spot for his bravery. Bad shoulder and all, he went on to serve out the war as a headquarters servant. Afterward he settled near Worcester, Massachusetts. His musket is displayed at the Bunker Hill Monument. Upon meeting an old matey, Peter Salem rendered a salute, according to historian Benson Lossing who interviewed many veterans. "Peter's right foot found its way into the hollow of the left, his body sprung erect, while his right hand sprang to the level of his eyes." Lossing remarked how Salem's black face screwed into a grimace registering the arthritic pain he suffered in that bad shoulder.

Without knowing it, Peter Salem, slave, single-handedly ushered in a new age of warfare, ending forever the pretense of chivalry in infantry combat. Perhaps it was symbolic that Major Pitcairn, champion of the haut monde, should be felled by a downtrodden slave.

At Brandywine, slave Private Edward Hector, 3d Pennsylvania Artillery, disobeyed the order to desert wagons and, firing abandoned weapons, was able to bring off his horses and wagon while whites fled in panic. Fifty years later, the grateful Pennsylvania legislature handed him a onetime thank you of $40.

Returning for a visit to America in 1824, Lafayette was struck by the changes and the increase in racial prejudice. He fondly recalled the days when black and white soldiers messed and fraternized and tramped and died side-by-side and were then rolled naked into mass graves. Now he found that whites were rarely seen with blacks unless the blacks were menials.

Lafayette complained sorrowfully that he came to aid America in its common fight for freedom of *all* mankind. When he pleaded with Jefferson, then in the last two years of his life, that freedom should begin by education, Jefferson agreed only in part. Blacks could learn to read print, he allowed, but not to write, for that would enable them to forge papers and therefore make it impossible to keep them subjugated.

# 2

# *Indians*

On April 1, 1775, weeks before the battle at Lexington, the Massachusetts Provincial Congress thanked Jehotakin Mtohksin of the Stockbridge Praying Indians for his willingness to take up the hatchet against redcoats. Thirty-four Indians were enlisted for the bonus of a blanket and a red ribbon. Jehotakin was also given a lieutenant's commission in Captain David Goodrich's company of Colonel John Patterson's Connecticut regiment.

Indians since Puritan days had assisted whites in combat against one tribe or another, usually as scouts, as against Canadian Abenakis that were led by French Jesuit priests in a century of border raids. Captain Sam Mott wrote to Governor Trumbull at the siege of Quebec City, telling how their Indian allies had learned to say proudly, "liberty," and how they pounded their chests and announced, "Me Yankee!" The Reverend William Emerson thought the sprawling camp at Cambridge "interesting," and mentioned the wigwams of 50 Stockbridge Praying Indians armed with bows, a few muskets, and ancient blunderbusses.

After Lexington, General Thomas Gage advised army headquarters in London, "We need not be tender of calling upon savages, as the Rebels have shown us the example by bringing as many Indians down against us as they could collect."

Gage was not speaking with forked tongue. Lord Dartmouth, at the urging of George III, instructed Colonel Guy Johnson of the British-American 50th Foot, alias Johnson's Greens, to entice Indians to "take up the hatchet against His Majesty's rebellious subjects in America."

Guy Johnson's father-in-law, Sir William Johnson, no relation, was created the third baron in America and given a huge estate he named Kingsborough. He became Superintendent of Indian Affairs after Pontiac's War and died on the eve of the War of Independence. For participating with the Six Nations, after the war the Johnsons forfeited the entire northern half of New York state.

To save face after their apparent forced evacuation from Boston, British agents explained to their Indian friends —

> *The King of England has subdued both France and Spain. Pray what can this handful in America do with such a king? The king is very subtle. He has deceived the Bostonians. He ordered his forces continued in Boston until the Bostonians had collected all the cannon that could be found, from*

*Philadelphia, New York and even from Virginia,
and brought to that place. The Bostonians,
having all their force and cannon collected, were
about to destroy the town but the king's officer
commanding there forbade them, telling them he
would leave it in a peaceful manner, as the pur-
pose of his coming there has now been answered.
And now, brother, you will soon hear that the
king's ships have laid waste to all their seaports,
as they can make no resistance, having sent all
their cannon and stores to Boston.*

Chevalier Samuel de Champlain was the first to expose American Indians to European combat when he successfully maneuvered his Algonquin Montagnais with mantelet (moveable shelters) against the palisaded "castles" of the Mohawks. "But," he wrote of his Hurons, "they are not soldiers. They do not want discipline or correction and only do what seems good for them."

Another reluctant employer of native Americans, Govern Jacque René de Brisay, Marquise de Demonville of New France, after a ten-day raid on the Senecas complained, "It is miserable business to command savages who, as soon as they have knocked an enemy on the head, ask for nothing but to go home and carry with him the scalp, which they take off like a skull cap."

In the French and Indian War (1757-63), Sir Jefferey Amherst became distrustful of Indians—

*A most idle worthless set. If I send them on scout
they all come back alive in twelve hours and here
they will do nothing but eat and drink, except
when forced to it.*

There was ample reason for white leaders to address American natives as "my children." Before learning the corrupt ways of Europeans, they were as guileless and as truthful as innocent children. At the beginning of the War of Independence, before huge tracts of their lands had been stolen or taken by treachery, their thoughts were simple and direct compared to those of artful white men. One diarist summed up their entire lack of sophistication in a single incident—

> *While some French officers were at dinner with His Excellency an Indian soldier entered the room, walked around the table and then stretched forth his long tattooed arm and seized a large joint of hot roast beef in his thumb and fingers, took it to the door, and began to eat it. General Washington gave orders that he was not to be interfered with, saying laughingly that it was apparently the dinner hour of this Mucius Scaevola of the New World.*

Scaevola (the left-handed) was the ancient Roman who, to show his lack of fear, thrust his right hand into a fire and held it there.

Washington spoke of the need to pity Indians: "They, poor wretches, have no Press through which their grievances are related, and it is well known that when one side only of a story is heard, and often repeated, the human mind becomes impressed with it, insensibly."

The 50 much-touted Oneidas of Captain Alan McLane's mounted Rough Riders, after impressing their fierce looks on the rest of the army, saw their first combat at Valley Forge. They were posted near Roxborough, Pennsylvania, as vedettes. Suddenly, catching sight of Howe's resplendent, brassy dragoons mounted on strutting thoroughbreds, the Oneidas were so frightened they broke and ran pell-mell without horses, stopping once to make a loud war whoop before heading for safety across the Schuykill River. Equally surprised at their first sight of wild painted Indians, the dragoons sat on their mounts staring in awe, forgetting to fire.

In the early days, natives treated the white man's war as a game. The story was told in northern New England of the frightened frontiersman who, as he ran out of his cabin waving a white flag, was ordered in broken English, "Go back to your house, we are going to fire at you." They had no strategy and their idea of a war was simply a series of raids on the weakest, most poorly guarded targets.

There were many reasons why Indians were not actively recruited by either side, and those who did recruit them were invariably disappointed. Colonel Benedict Arnold signed up 50 Abenakis on his trek to Quebec, cutting across the vast wilderness of northern Maine into Canada for "one Portuguese per month with two Spanish dollars bonus, provision and liberty to choose their own officers." Before one shot was fired, they assumed another liberty. They bugged out en masse, a slippery maneuver that was always an Indian's privilege.

Mediocre at waging real war as opposed to raiding, native Americans found their greatest value in man-to-man combat. With no importance attached to accumulation of materials, proof of manhood was an Indian's only route to personal success. In this act, the death of an enemy by itself was of no great value, militarily or otherwise. It was the supreme show of manhood that counted—primitive machismo. It wasn't that Indians were cowardly (even by white man's definition); it was ridiculous not to pick the opportunity when the odds were high in one's favor—an unguarded isolated family, say.

Death in battle held no glory to eastern American Indians; such a personal way of being defeated was a peculiar whim of white man. That he was brave, the Indian proved to himself and friends by self-inflicted punishments.

It was not that there was a great technological gulf between whites and natives; the original Quakers of Pennsylvania huddled like animals in caves during their first few years in America, with less than the bark and animal fur protection of the natives. This same convenience, burrowing into the side of steep hills for winter protection, was responsible for original Wisconsinites earning the nickname badgers.

Little metal had been cast anywhere in the world by 1775, and utensils of the whites were fabricated almost as crudely as those of the natives. The only truly unique invention was the clock. Even the harquebus, with all its noise and smoke, was often inferior to bows and arrows. As late as 1776, Benjamin Franklin seriously proposed bows, arrows and pikes (spears) for the many advantages they possessed over firearms.

Neither the Age of Reason nor its offshoot, the Industrial Age, had made much headway in America, and there was little technological separation, none that an intelligent native could not have crossed quite easily. Had the natives assimilated the technology of Europeans as did the Japanese in the Meiji era, the story of conquest in North America might have been much different.

On the plus side, the American natives did not have to be conscripted or trained to go on combat raids, nor were they ever threatened with anything other than shame should they hold back. In most tribes, until a man was successful on the warpath and proved himself before an armed enemy, he was known by a familiar baby name. One who for any reason refused to fight, was physically incapable (very rare among natives), or misbehaved in combat, retained his baby name and remained the rest of his life among women or until he proved himself a man. Sometimes he was given a woman's name.

The initial decision to raid made by the chief, with the council of elderly advisors, was announced at a pow-wow, brought on by an outstanding leader, who might or might not be the chief. He did so knowing full well that he would be held personally responsible for the outcome. Disgrace went to the Indian who talked big and lost heavily. War leaders of the Six Nations began matters by driving their tomahawks into the war post in the center of the village and dancing about it, drumming and chanting for others to volunteer. It was a sacred ceremony beginning with cleansing oneself with herb emetics and fasting, as well as practicing continence. He who would join the war party stepped forth declaring loudly what great things he would do.

Instead of accepting subordinate roles as do white men, one Indian had as much to say as any other, although he usually deferred to age and experience. Daubed with gaudy, fearsome (they hoped) war paint, glistening with bear grease, they harangued back and forth, one stimulating another as each made service vows that could not be lightly broken. "I, Swamp Flower, will kill two Yankees!" one uninitiated young brave might boast, then proclaim confidence in his war-party leader, show utter lack of concern for his own safety and, finally, prepare for the worst by chanting his chosen death song.

In preparing for a raid, a would-be leader threw a bundle of sticks on the ground to be proudly retrieved by volunteers. Those who survived the raid wore their stick of valor around their necks, as valid a symbol to them as the Medal of Honor. Red Stick Creek Indians of the deep South got their nickname preceding the War of 1812 by retrieving sticks painted red by Tecumseh to enlist their tribe in the common cause.

Next to raw courage, the biggest advantage an Indian had was being unencumbered on the march and in battle, often his undoing. Captain John Smith of Jamestown, Virginia, complained, "For the savages are so light and swift though we see them, being so laden with armor, they have much advantage over us, though they be cowards." Smith knew that all he had to do was to button up and survive the first few onslaughts, after which he could attack, for the natives would be out of arrows or soon enough have to leave on their own accord, being out of food, water and enthusiasm.

Native Americans refused to fight for either side at Freeman's Farm, but after darkness fell over the battlefield, they crept about scalping the heroic dead, British and American. Nor were Indians the clever, stalwart, stealthy, seemingly unbeatable fighters that such popular writers as James Fenimore Cooper made them out to be.

Mostly they were lousy, literally and figuratively, undependable berserkers unworthy of the name soldier, much too undisciplined to know what personal sacrifice was.

General Karl von Clausewitz, in his three-volume *Von Kriege*, observed that combat is the realm of confusion. With Indians, command was a nightmare in or out of combat, and it is a great fallacy that they were always as alert as the creatures of the wild.

The Loyalist Queen's Rangers, New York men, on August 31, 1778, surprised and overran an Indian outpost north of the town entrusted to the care of Daniel Nina of the Wappinger tribe, Chief of the Stockbridge Indians. In that affair, the Valentine Hill Massacre, or Indian Bridge, two natives survived. British-led Indians of the Six Nations lost a battle at Newtown (Elmira, New York) because, having waited in ambush eight days for General Sullivan's column, their camouflage was so wilted they were observed a mile away.

Once battle got underway, they fought as individuals, emotional and mercurial. According to Sir Guy Carlton, Canadian governor, "They are easily dejected and choose to be on the strongest side, so that, when they are most wanted, they vanish."

Except for a strip of cloth passed through a belt to cover their genitals, the natives were naked during much of the mild months. One missionary described them—

*Imagine a great assembly of savages adorned with every ornament most suited to disfigure them in European eyes, painted with vermilion, white, green, yellow and black, methodically laid on with the help of a little tallow. The head is shaved except for the top, where there is a small tuft, to which are fastened feathers, a few beads of wampum or some trinket. Pendants hang from their noses and also from their ears, which are split in infancy and drawn with weights until they flap at last against the shoulders.*

Governor William Byrd I, like many provincials, held Indian marksmanship in utter contempt and justified his selling them muskets by noting what poor shots they were. Their aim with bows and arrows at close range, however, was often deadly. To conserve precious gunpowder, Indians would charge their guns with so little powder that colonists could tell when a native fired from the weakness of the sound.

An Indian whipped up to killing pitch didn't wait, didn't even want to know the difference between a Scotch Loyalist and a backwoods Rebel. That he was white was enough for him. Civilized Europeans, however, carefully stylized wholesale murder neatly into the categories honorable and dishonorable, fair and unfair. On this scale, Indian marauds were unacceptable. Campaigning against Indians was arduous work, and General Horatio Gates turned down such a command, apologizing to General Washington, "The man who understands Indian service should enjoy youth and strength; requisites I do not possess. It therefore grieves me that your excellency should offer me the only command to which I am entirely unequal." Gates, too, had served with Braddock. The difficult command was finally accepted by General John Sullivan, whose favorite toast thereafter was, "May the enemies of America be metamorphosed into pack horses and sent on a western expedition against the Indians."

Earning the nickname, the Town Destroyer, which he shared with General Washington, Sullivan burned or carried off everything in sight. Although he killed few braves, moving slowly enough to give them plenty of time to evade, he cut down orchards and burned Iroquois long houses, a maraud for which isolated settlers paid dearly.

Americans, especially, hated the tomahawk, believing that when you got that close to a superior enemy you deserved the courtesy of being allowed to surrender, and by employing Indians the British lost much caste among Europe's ruling class. Typical was the reaction of Spaniard Martin Navarro, in this note to Bernardo de Gálvez (Galveston, Texas) —

> *While we are under the belief that the English had been falsely charged with the atrocities committed in North America upon persons of all classes by the hands of the various savage tribes who followed their banners, there was given a most amazing proof of the fact by Captain Hesse at the head of three hundred regular troops and nine hundred savages which left not the least doubt that this nation has forgotten how to make war according to the system practiced in Europe.*

The journal of Erkuries Beatty, who, in October 1779, served in Sullivan's 4,000-man campaign in New York's Finger Lakes, tells us why and how Indians were used as terror weapons —

> *On entering Genessee we found the body of Lieutenant Boyd and another rifleman in a most terrible mangled condition. They were both stripped naked and their heads cut off and the flesh of Lieutenant Boyd's head was entirely taken off and his eyes punched out. The other man's head was not there. They were stabbed, I suppose, in forty different places in the body with a spear and great gashes cut in their flesh with knives and Lieutenant Boyd's privates was nearly cut off and hanging down, his finger and toenails was bruised off and the dogs had eat part of their shoulders away; likewise a knife was sticking in Lieutenant Boyd's body. They was immediately buried with the honors of war.*

Savage, uncalled-for use of the white weapon, the bayonet, was made a number of times by battle-frenzied Scotch and border Britishers — as when Lieutenant Colonel Isaac Ledyard of Connecticut was run through with his own sword, trying to surrender. Fort Griswold at New London was burned to the ground in this Arnold-led raid. Ledyard and 88 militiamen were massacred while trying to surrender. In another affair, Brigadier General Hugh Mercer was bayoneted unmercifully simply because, when disarmed, he refused to say he surrendered.

Lieutenant Thomas Boyd and his sergeant were tortured and, according to an escapee, Chief Joseph Brant, though raised in the Masons by George III himself,

[38]

refused to heed Boyd's Freemason distress signal. When the regiment passed the lonely graves on the return march, Colonel Thomas Proctor ordered the musicians to play "Rosyln Castle," "the soft and mocking notes of which cast a hush over the regiment and awakened pity for their comrades." A shrine in a small state park near Genesco, New York, on U.S. Route 20A is dedicated to Lieutenant Thomas Boyd and Sergeant Joshua Parker.

Indians were not alone in committing outrages. Four companies of Dan Morgan's wild riflemen with Sullivan's column captured one Oneida Indian community, part of the Six Nations in the Finger Lake district of central New York. These Virginia Long Knives added disgust to the terror of their name by gang-raping and slitting the throats of helpless squaws, young and old. A Lieutenant William Barton of the 1st New Jersey recorded proudly in his diary how Indians were tortured for hours, being peeled alive for their skin to make boot legs.

In Prince Philip's War in 1675, Reverend Solomon Stoddard of Northhampton, Massachusetts, suggested that English hunt American natives with "dogs, as they do bears and wolves," as the Spaniards did, as slave-owners hunted their runaway property, and as they did all along in Virginia. He reminded his fellow Christians —

> *If ye Indians were as other people and did manage their war fairly after ye manner of other nations, it might be looked upon as inhumane to pursue them in such manner, but they do acts of hostilities without proclaiming war. They don't appear openly in ye field to bid us battle; they use those*

*cruelly that fall into their hands; they act like*
*wolves and are to be dealt with as wolves.*

The first atrocity of the War of Independence did not involve Indians, only a frightened Yankee teenager who worked for Reverend William Emerson. He ran out on the bridge at Concord and brained a wounded British soldier with a hatchet. Reverend Emerson, on the scene that day with a musket, wrote, "The poor object lived an hour or two before he expired." Rumor spread through the British ranks that Americans were scalping captives and there was no reason to doubt this.

General Washington once sent the badly mutilated body of a young American lieutenant under a flag of truce to show Cornwallis the results of the unbridled savagery of some of his men. It was returned forthwith with a characteristic Cornwallis reply that he, the Marquis Cornwallis, was no coroner. Later, the bayoneting of defenseless, sleeping, American soldiers at Paoli Inn, Pennsylvania, was an excuse for retaliation against helpless British wounded prisoners of war at Germantown.

In October 1778, angered by the French Alliance, Great Britain announced an all-out war against the Rebels. Lord George Germain insisted that, by allying with Britain's traditional foe, Americans were identical to the French and must be treated the same. As the Ministry announced all-out war, Lord Suffolk appealed to the bench of bishops, "There is an article in the extraordinaries of the army for scalping knives. Great Britain defeats any hope in the justice of her cause by means like these to support it."

This "war of desolation," as the British Ministers

called it, resulted in raids on coastal cities and in the infamous Wyoming (Pennsylvania) and Cherry Valley (New York) Indian massacres. Indian outrages were the best aid American recruiters could get, engendering more hatred for the British than anything the enemy had ever done.

Scalping is described by Jacob Dievendorff of Palatine Bridge, New York, who, since he survived the process, was an authority. Take the scalping knife, as large as the Bowie knife, he told historian Benson Lossing, and make an incision at the hairline along the forehead and around the head in a circle. Should the hair be short, the scalper raised the skin on the forehead, took hold of it with his teeth and tore the scalp away from the bared thin flesh covering the skull. Females and men with long hair were easier, after making his circular cut merely twist the hair around one hand and with a sudden jerk lift the scalp neatly off the dome. Indians were frustrated by bald men and sometimes mutilated their faces in rage. Bearded men confused them, and short-cropped blacks, the buffalo soldiers later out West, were left unshorn.

The scalp was scraped of flesh and tanned as one would any animal pelt. It was often marked in such a way that its proud owner could remember when, where and how he got it. Robert Rogers, a ranger, found more than 800 scalps at the head village of the Canadian St. Francis Abenaki and other associated Algonquins. More recent ones were stretched over hoops of willow wood and some comically painted.

Nothing, not even the use of mercenaries, so infuriated frontiersmen as when the British unleashed Indians on their unprotected families while the frontiersmen were serving hundreds of miles away. More than any other irritation it caused the second war with Britain in 1812. Fear of savages and hatred for those who encouraged the savages' sly murderous attacks was clearly enunciated in a passage of the Declaration of Independence —

*He has excited domestic insurrection among us, and has endeavored to bring on the inhabitants of our frontiers the merciless Indian savages, whose known rules of warfare is an indistinguishable destruction of all ages, sexes and conditions.*

Despite objections by Canada's royal governor, the erstwhile playwright Gentleman Johnny Burgoyne used Indians as a terror weapon. "Let not people consider their distance from my camp," he threatened in broadsides nailed to trees near English settlements. "I have but to give stretch to the Indian forces under my direction, and they amount to thousands, to overtake the hardened enemies of Great Britain."

Actually, he had no more than 600 independent Indians. Nevertheless, one-third of the population of Cherry and Mohawk Valleys in northern New York were killed or dragged away as prisoners. Another third deserted to the Loyalists, and the remainder moved away. Twenty-four forts, some of them merely reinforced stone farmhouses, were built across the desolate land on a 63-mile front from Schenectady to German Flats.

However, Indians got their belly full of pitched battle at Oriskany. After standing up to the Rebels that one time, they reverted to their custom of sneaking up on helpless settlers.

Lieutenant Governor of Canada, Henry Hamilton, commander of the small garrison of British regulars at Detroit, made an evil reputation throughout the frontier as the Hair-Buyer. It was a matter of public record that by July 1777, Hamilton's parties had brought in 73 prisoners and 129 scalps.

That was not as bad, though, as the British squawman deserter, David Owens, who turned in the scalps of his wife and four children for a Pennsylvania bounty, nor as disgusting as the French officers of early-day Louisiana who profited by selling the offspring of their Indian slave women — their own mixed flesh and blood.

In London, Ben Franklin added propaganda fuel to the hatred by shocking the British public with a cleverly forged letter telling of the English under Hamilton buying "bales of American scalps, including women and children, from the Indians." Exact figures have a way of sounding authentic, and so one of Franklin's bales "contained the scalps of 43 soldiers, 297 farmers (some burned alive or surprised in the night), 67 old people, 88 women (some designated mothers), 193 boys, 211 girls, 29 little infants of various sizes, and other too mutilated to classify."

American and British alike used Indians if and whenever they could, practicality being the only scruple. To ease their conscience and to discourage scalping, both sides offered generous rewards for live prisoners. Congress gave $100 for a live British or Loyalist officer and $30 for a private.

Washington, despite bitter experience with Indian

allies in the French and Indian War, was not adverse to using Indians, but on the other hand, he never pushed for their recruitment. British use of Indians in northern New York was as costly as in the Southern Department where isolated outrages of the Creeks, Cherokees and Catawbas did more to unify the Rebels than any tax law of Parliament and caused hundreds of formerly luke-warm Loyalists to turn against the Crown.

Rebels, noting that Indians waited behind trees until a militiaman fired his musket and then darted forward with tomahawk and scalping knife, learned early to form two-man teams, fighting back-to-back, one ready to fire as the other reloaded.

An especially great demoralizer among Dan Morgan's "exterminating riflemen" was Private Timothy Murphy's double-barreled rifle, which the Indians respectfully referred to as "the gun that speaks twice." This barrel-over-barrel weapon was made by James Glocher of Easton, Pennsylvania, one of the best gunsmiths of the time.

Muskets were blazing away from both sides at Oriskany Falls when a violent summer storm put a temporary halt to the slaughter. Both sides retired a short distance away as though by agreement. Many of the Indians took that as a signal to slink away, particularly those who felt they had made coup, anxious to get home to do some bragging. The whites, when their flash pans were dry enough to keep sparks alive, returned to the affray and soon carried the day. It was one of the bloodiest battles of the war. Of 700 Rebels, 200 were killed outright, wounded or missing.

The final maneuver was an aggressive bayonet

charge urged on by the mortally wounded Brigadier General Nicholas Herkimer (originally Ergeshimer), who, knowing he would die, had one of his soldiers retrieve his amputated leg and lay it beside him so he might appear whole in Valhalla. Herkimer had been commissioned a lieutenant of militia in Schenectady in January 1758, in the French and Indian War. In 1775, he had been appointed colonel of the First Battalion of Tryon (later Herkimer) County militia, and a brigadier general a year later.

Long battles were difficult to sustain under the best weather conditions because muskets and rifles after comparatively few firings, depending on the quality of gunpowder, became so clogged with ash it was impossible to ram balls home. Soldiers would piss into the barrels to dissolve the residue, but with or without solvent, it took time to clean the barrels.

Often a piece would fail to fire because a clogged vent hole interrupted the powder train from the flash pan into the barrel chamber, at which the soldier was a flash in the pan. Soldiers carried vent pricks, like short hat pins, stuck in their jacket collars, to clean the vent holes. They also carried two wooden tampions, one to plug the muzzle and the other to plug the vent, to keep them clean and dry when not in use.

Because New England and northern New York militias so feared Indians, whom their ancestors had battled over a century, they were slow answering General Philip Schuyler's call to help stop General Burgoyne's advance. Burgoyne's forces included his Canadian militia, red-coated regulars, German mercenaries, Hurons, Wyandots, Abenaki and other Algonquins, as well as renegade Onondagas, Mohawks, Oneidas and others of the Iroquois Six Nations.

Not until Dan Morgan's wild shirt men came dog-trotting up from Morristown, New Jersey, did citizens of the threatened area begin slowly to muster. The wild appearance of these hard-drinking, cussing, tobacco-chawing frontiersmen, the famed accuracy of their long rifles, their habit of carrying rifle balls in their mouths to quench their thirst and for faster reloading, and their eerie wild turkey calls had the same effect on northern Indians that those Indians had on civilized eastern whites.

The Six Iroquois Nations, at first pledged neutrality to both sides, and since it was more to the Rebels' advantage for them to remain neutral, the Rebels worked harder at it than the British. By 1776, however, Congress reversed its policy authorizing General Washington to enlist up to 2,000 Indians as a reserve for the Northern Department. Aside from individuals accepted to fill quotas, that was never accomplished. One volunteer who remained to be assimilated into the Continental Line, Lewis Atayatoghwongthta, became a lieutenant colonel.

Dr. Albigence Waldo noted at Valley Forge, "I was called to relieve a soldier thought to be dying. He expired before I reached the hut. He was an Indian, an excellent soldier and an obedient, good-natured fellow. He has fought for those very people who disinherited his forefathers."

# 3

# *Women*

The butchered bodies of eight women were found among the debris of Braddock's army in 1755. Women have died beside or in support of soldiers in all America's wars and seldom given their due. Historians, often from stuffy academia to begin with, take little interest in the subject matter and if they mention women at all in reference to combat, they do so with as much derogation as others did with blacks and Indians.

In a letter before the Declaration of Independence was announced, Abigail Adams threatened her husband John —

> *In the new code of laws which I suppose it will be necessary for you to make, I desire you would remember the ladies, and be more generous to them than your ancestors. Do not put such unlimited power in the hands of husbands. Remember, all men would be tyrants if they could. If particular*

*care and attention are not paid to the ladies, we*
*are determined to foment a rebellion, and will*
*not hold ourselves bound to obey the laws in*
*which we have no voice or representation.*

On the other hand, the proud author of "all men are created equal," the redhead Thomas Jefferson, while avoiding battles, gave this patronizing advice to the fair sex —

*Do not be too wise to wrinkle your foreheads*
*with politics.*

Women performed a number of dangerous deeds during the War of Independence. At the furious, no-quarter battle of Saratoga, the wife of a British soldier made repeated trips for water for the wounded. Several soldiers had been killed at the zeroed-in spring, and though American riflemen withheld fire on her first trip, there was no guarantee all would continue to do so. After it was over, according to Madame Frederica Riedesel, grateful soldiers "threw whole handfuls of coins into this brave woman's lap."

Molly Pitcher Hays (neé Ludwig) was Sergeant Molly to the admiring soldiers whom she inspired in the heat of combat. Her sergeant's warrant was signed by General Washington, and for her they added a new stanza to "Yankee Doodle" —

*Molly Pitcher she stood by her gun*
*An rammed the charges home, sir,*
*And thus on Monmouth's bloody field,*
*A sergeant did become, sir.*

Popular though she was with the men beside whom she fought, the battlefield deed she performed, carrying water in a pitcher repeatedly to cool over-heated cannon barrels at Monmouth, went unrecognized by Congress. Not until 1822, at age 68, did Mrs. Pitcher Hayes receive the first payment of a $40-a-year pension voted by Pennsylvania many years earlier. As time went by, her second marriage soured and she began to drink heavily and act the tough artillery sergeant, chawing tobacco, swearing like any trooper, dying at 78 among soldier maties.

Another Molly was just as famous. Those who survived the furious battle at Fort Washington along the Hudson River sang the deeds of no man, but those of the war volunteer Margaret "Molly" Corbin. Molly was no stranger to combat, having survived an Indian raid on the Pennsylvania frontier in which she lost her mother, father and brothers. Alone in the world, she followed her husband, a matros (cannon gunner's assistant) in the 1st Company of Pennsylvania artillery, to New York. When he was killed by heavy preparatory fire, she took up his rammer staff and went on sponging and ramming until she was badly wounded.

Hessians found her nearly dead, abandoned on the battlefield beside her cannon. Like an Amazon of old, one breast was demolished by grapeshot, but the Hessians took good care of that brave soldier woman.

A fixture at the Invalid Corps at West Point for many years, Captain Molly, as young cadets called her respectfully (and behind her back, Dirty Kate, in her husband's tattered old artillery coat), would good-naturedly return the salutes of untested boys. In 1799, Congress granted her a pension equal to half a matros's pay and a new suit of clothes every year. That was another promise Congress never kept. Molly lies with other heroes in the soldier's cemetery at the West Point Military Academy.

Prior to 1788, no medical examination was given to recruits, which, of course, made it much easier for women to join the ranks. Among an unknown number of women combatants was Deborah Sampson Gannett, abandoned as a baby and raised as a hired girl by a Middlesboro, Massachusetts, family. One popular but unsubstantiated version has her a black slave owned by that family. In any event, in 1781, she borrowed a suit of clothes from one Sam Leonard and joined under the alias of an acquaintance, Timothy Thayer, who had been killed in combat on Long Island.

Discovered after several weeks, she was forced to return her enlistment bonus and was kicked out of the Army. She then walked 75 miles to Worchester, Massachusetts, and enlisted in Captain George Webb's company of the 4th Massachusetts under the alias of Robert Surtlieff. With several battles, including Yorktown, behind her, in a skirmish in May 1782, at Westchester, New York, she was cut in the face by a saber and caught a musket ball in her shoulder.

Her sex was not discovered even then, but later during a bout with yellow fever, a surgeon found her out and rather than thank her for her service, saw to it that she was summarily discharged. Later at Washington's urging, Congress voted her a small pension and a grant of land and she was allowed to remain in the Corps of Invalids at West Point.

Her story was published in 1797 in the *Female Review*. She married Benjamin Gannett and became the mother of two daughters, Mary and Patience, and a son Earl. In 1802, she became the first woman lecturer in America, touring the northern states in full Continental uniform, beginning her talks with brisk run-throughs of the manual of arms for the musket, despite her bad shoulder. When she died in 1827, at 67, her husband received $80 a month widower's pension, and in World War II one of the Liberty ships was named the *Deborah Sampson*.

Down South was Nancy Hart, terror of Georgia Loyalists, six foot, big-boned, "unmannered and masculine" and, although cross-eyed, an expert shot.

Among the unsung *filles du regiment* were women whom George Washington proudly tolerated. On the pass-in-review parade in Philadelphia prior to Yorktown, he put out the order for all women to bring up the rear, along with camp kettles and other impedimenta. American camp followers have been pictured as whores, known as "exchange wenches." Perhaps many were, but even they performed an honest service, which two-thirds of Americans failed to do.

Unknown to history books, the good women of Philadelphia brought into Valley Forge on January 7, 1778, at great risk—

> *Ten teams of oxen for slaughter, driven by patriotic women who also brought in two thousand shirts, smuggled out of the city, sewn under the eyes of the enemy.*

Martha Washington and the wives of a number of

senior staff officers, such as Lucy Knox and General Greene's pretty young bride, Catherine Littlefield Greene, with their infant son George Washington Greene, followed their men and comforted them in winter quarters. Wives and sweethearts of lower ranks, as the two heroic Mollies, certainly were more than prostitutes.

In the spring of 1778, at Valley Forge, wives and children of some of the Pennsylvania soldiers resided in camp for a time. One, 11-year-old John Geyer, stayed on as a drummer boy and, like his dad, was twice wounded before it was over.

Women suffered in ways male soldiers were immune to. Lord Cornwallis's long-awaited home leave was canceled by the Trenton raid, and his wife died before she could see him again. Jeminia Tullekens, Lady Cornwallis, typifies the quiet desperation of soldiers' wives. Because of the many and long separations from the man she loved, she asked that a thorn bush be planted on her grave, "as nearly over my heart as possible."

While John was safe in Philadelphia that first year, Abigail Adams was alone with the children in enemy-occupied Boston, her house marked with a large R for Rebel. She lived near enough to the trajectories of cannon from Breed's Hill that at any time a stray round might have killed her and the kids. She told her diary—

> *I went to bed about twelve, and rose again a little*
> *after one. I could no more sleep than if I had been*
> *in the engagement; the rattling of the windows,*
> *the jar of the house, the continual roar of twenty-*
> *four pounders; and the bursting of the shells give*

*us such ideas, and realize a scene to us of which*
*we could form scarcely any conception.*

John, as most patriotic husbands, appreciated the silent courage of his loved ones. Remembering the years of hardships Abigail had cheerfully undergone alone, how she had done a man's work on the farm, had fed and clothed and trained the children, had kept the home intact, he wrote to her —

> *You are really brave, my dear. You are a heroine*
> *and you have reason to be, for the worst that can*
> *happen can do you no harm. A soul as pure, as*
> *benevolent, as virtuous, and pious as yours has*
> *nothing to fear, but everything to hope from the*
> *last of human evils.*

Doctor James Craig wrote to Dr. Potts, Purveyor General for Hospitals, on May 1, 1778 —

> *The General desires orderlies [hospital orderlies,*
> *men pulled from the regiments to assist in the*
> *general hospitals] to rejoin their regiments by*
> *the first of June, and we have already had some*
> *scuffling with several colonies about them. I*
> *wish some method could be fallen upon to em-*
> *ploy women that can be depended on. The Gen-*
> *eral says one may enlist them for at least the*
> *same money as are paid soldiers, for we can no*
> *longer bear having an army on paper and not*
> *have them in the field.*

Women at war got into their share of trouble, as

[53]

this New Jersey regimental order indicates —

*Whereas some women of the brigade have be-*
*haved in the most infamous manner, they may*
*be assured that upon the first complaint made*
*against them, their ration will be stopped and*
*they banished from the camp.*

Private Caleb Haskell tells in his diary of an experience he had at the Cambridge Camp —

*I went to Watertown to see some cannon and*
*mortars that were brought in; this afternoon*
*there was a man whipped and drummed out of*
*the army for stealing ... came off guard this*
*morning. Was paraded in the Common in the*
*afternoon. All still in the camp ... our army is in*
*high spirits.... This morning a bad woman was*
*taken up in the camp, in the afternoon was*
*doused in the river and drummed out of town.*

General Nathaniel Greene once ordered a woman
convicted of carrying a message to British General Howe
to be given 100 lashes and drummed out of camp. She
would have been executed had she been a man.

A woman's ration was half that of a man, and the
few children authorized to accompany the Army, usually
only in the artillery, drew a fourth that of a soldier. The
mild curse, I'll be a son-of-a-gun (cannon), by the way,
began in Europe in the early 1500s when artillerymen's
sons were born on a campaign.

Women were safe when captured in the field by

eastern Indians, for these natives subscribed to the belief of the Six Nations that continence must be practiced on the warpath in order to maintain strength. Many white women after a few months preferred to remain with their captors. What occurred when they were finally exchanged or returned at war's ending, as in the French and Indian War, was very difficult for those at home to understand. As far as frontier life was concerned, in the 18th and 19th centuries, it wasn't that much different. It is difficult, however, for civilized folk to imagine a captured white woman finding her new life with savages so appealing.

Women were as safe from the majority of disciplined British regulars and their not so disciplined German allies as they were from American soldiers, which means, of course, there were exceptions.

During the occupation of Boston before the war, Sam Adams and cohorts fabricated inferences that women were being violated by British soldiers, but never gave names and details. If it happened, it was never a matter of record and one can be sure that Sam and his ace propagandists would have spelled out the dirtiest details and made it a matter of common knowledge had it occurred. Perhaps as a Congressional rape investigation committee reported, there were careless women, but evidently the acts "were not violent enough to them to have complained." One British officer did complain—

*The infamous falsehoods they circulate in their papers which we sometimes see, relative to the behavior of our army and navy fill me with indignation.... These misrepresentations may perhaps*

[55]

*influence the spirits of the lower class against
the troops, but they will have a most pernicious
effect when our men are let slip against a parcel
of wretches whom they hate and despise, when
no officers will interfere to rescue the victim
from their rage.*

Considering the large number of convicted felons in the British Army, and there was listed at the time some 300, the number and seriousness of offenses committed by regulars was remarkably small, which speaks well for the discipline imposed by officers and sergeants. Rest assured, however, anti-British newspapers in Boston exploited every incident, the worst discovered after searching early accounts being —

*A worthy gentleman the other morning discov-
ered a soldier in bed with a favorite granddaugh-
ter. The aged parent in the height of his astonish-
ment ordered the soldier immediately to quit the
room. It was found that the soldier had found
means to ingratiate himself with one of the family
and had by her aid seduced the girl with the
promise of marriage. That, accordingly, one eve-
ning as the girl informs, he carried her to the
house in town where as she thought they were
married by a person dressed as a priest. But how
it must increase our detestation of the present
measures to find that not only the magistrates of
this metropolis are insulted with impunity, but
that the most dear and tender connections must be
broken and violated. We should not wish to draw*

*invidious comparisons but surely if in the arbi-*
*trary reign of a Stuart, the quartering of a*
*standing army in the time of peace upon the in-*
*habitants of a town are deemed a grievance....*

The British swore there was no need to force women in Boston for "there is not an officer or private down to a drummer that cannot have his bedfellow for the winter; so that the Yankee war, contrary to all others, will produce more births than burials."

One Congressional committee appointed in 1777 to investigate the conduct of enemy soldiers in the Jerseys reported in part—

*... the lust and brutality of the soldiers in abusing*
*women. The Committee has authentic information*
*of many instances of the most indecent treatment*
*and actual ravishment of married and single*
*women; but such is the nature of that most irrepa-*
*rable injury that the persons suffering it, though*
*perfectly innocent, look upon it as a kind of re-*
*proach to have the facts and their names known.*
*Some complaints were made to the commanding*
*officers on this subject, and one affidavit made*
*before a justice of the peace but it could not learn*
*that any satisfaction was ever given or punish-*
*ment inflicted, except that one soldier in Benning-*
*ton was kept in custody for part of a day.*

One British officer recorded in his diary during the occupation of Boston before the war, "The women are very handsome, but, like old mother Eve, very frail,"

Frail was used as in the second dictionary definition: liable to fall from virtue. "Our camp has been well supplied in that way since we have been on Boston Common, as if our tents were pitched on Black Heath." Black Heath, an elevated commons in southeast London, was notorious for the after-dark activities of loose women.

At age 25, Lord Francis Rawdon from County Down, Ireland, reputed to be the ugliest man in Great Britain, commanded the Volunteers of Ireland and wrote to his friend the Earl of Huntington from Staten Island in 1776, right after it was captured —

> *The fair nymphs of this isle are in wonderful tribulation, as the fresh meat our men have got here has made them riotous as satyrs. A girl cannot step into the bushes to pluck a rose without running the most imminent risk of being ravished, and they are so little accustomed to these vigorous methods that they don't bear them with the proper resignation, and of consequence we have the most entertaining courts-martial every day.*
>
> *To the southward they behaved much better in these cases, if I may judge from a woman who having been forced by seven of our men made a complaint to me, not on her usage, she said, no, thank God, she despised that, but of their having taken an old prayer book for which she had a particular affection.*
>
> *A girl on the island made a complaint the other day to Lord Percy of her being deflowered, as she said, by some grenadiers. Lord Percy asked her how she knew them to be grenadiers as it*

*happened in the dark. "Oh good God," cried she,*
*"they could be nothing else, and if your Lordship*
*will examine them I am sure you will find it so."*

A British soldier of the lower ranks needed written permission to marry and that occurred only when the woman would be of special use to the service, such as a washerwoman. To augment what little subsistence they could get from their husbands, women sometimes sold themselves along with whiskey and rum. Such women were tolerated because they were known to be capable nurses in combat when, of course, every whore was an angel from heaven.

In the Continental Army, female camp followers not married to soldiers were ordered periodically to a hospital to be examined for venereal disease.

During the British occupation, for stealing a jug of rum, one British private's woman was sentenced to a hundred lashes at a cart's tail and marched through the center of Boston stripped to the waist. Proper Bostonians must have approved, for that is exactly what they did to Quaker women who refused to be intimidated.

In the South, Cornwallis discovered that camp followers were the most aggressive looters. In an effort to curb looting, he had them fall in at the rear during roll calls, where they were forced to witness all floggings and executions.

Before every battle, capable women were recruited as unpaid volunteers. Women got together in bandage-rolling bees to prepare lint and linen bandages. Some 2,000 bandages were rolled for Washington's men as they anticipated a British attack on Dorcester Heights outside

Boston. Fortunately, the enemy evacuated Boston before they were needed.

Washington tried on several occasions to enlist women as permanent paid nurses in several army hospitals. In general orders on June 17, 1777, at Middle Brook—

> *A proportionate number of women to the sick of each regiment, shall be sent to the hospital in Mendham and Black River to attend the sick as nurses.*

Food being very scarce in Boston during the siege, the British put out the order—

> *Any woman who may be wanted as a nurse at the General Hospital or to do any other business for the service of the garrison and shall refuse to do it, will immediately be struck from the provision list.*

The British Expeditionary Force carried three washerwomen per musket company, a necessity if only because of the white lace and colorful facings, and allowed a certain number of camp followers. No provision was made by the Continental Army for women although unrecognized 'ammunition wives' would double in combat as nurses. This was attested to in an unusually blunt reference in a General Order at Valley Forge for 18 April 1778—

> *The camp whores, who have now become numerous, are being used as nurses.*

# 4

# *Children and Old Men*

The fact was that after the first two years of the War of Independence, a few truly tough professional combat soldiers began to appear in the American Army. Hard campaigning was rapidly separating men from boys, no matter what their race. Nor were all the 'men' out of their middle teens, nor all 'boys' so young in experience. Washington's men, black and white, young, old, or crippled were standing up to be counted. Captain Schlozer, with the Germans in the Battle of Saratoga, noted in his book, *Briefe aus Neu England* —

> *English America surpasses the most of Europe in the growth and looks of its male population. The whole nation has a natural turn and talent for war and a soldier's life.... We passed through the American camp in which all the regiments were drawn up beside the artillery, and stood under*

*arms. Not one of them was uniformly clad; each had on the clothes which he wore in the fields, the church or the tavern. They stood, however, like soldiers, well-arranged and with a military air. There were regular regiments also, which, for want of time and cloth were not yet equipped in uniform. These had standards with various emblems and mottos, some of which had for us a very satirical significance.*

Germans were impressed by American soldiers all the more so for what they lacked. "You cannot find a man of 30 who has not borne arms," wrote Baron de Closen. "I admire the American troops tremendously! It is incredible that soldiers composed even of children of 15, of whites and blacks, almost naked, unpaid and rather poorly fed, can march so well and withstand fire so steadfastly."

French officer Claude Blanchard saw "some fine-looking men; also many who are small and thin, and even some children 12 or 13 years old. They have no uniform and in general are badly clad."

"I cannot insist too strongly," wrote Baron du Bourg, "how I was surprised by the American Army. It is truly incredible that troops almost naked, poorly paid and composed of old men and children and Negroes should behave so well on the march under fire."

Abbe Claude Robin, chaplain of the French Soissonais Regiment, noted, "I am astonished at finding in their tents, where three or four men live, not over 40 pounds of baggage. Hardly any of them have a mattress. One blanket spread over branches and the bark of trees serves their officers as a bed."

Gentleman Johnny Burgoyne, too, was amazed and as a POW wrote Lord Germain —

*I should now hold myself unjustifiable if I did not confide to your lordship my opinion upon a near Inspection of the rebel troops. The standing corps which I have seen are disciplined. I do not hazard the term but apply it to the great fundamental points of military institution, sobriety, subordination, regularity and courage. The militia are inferior in method and movement, but not a jot less serviceable in the woods. The panic of the rebel troops is confined.*

Printed in the United States
125994LV00002B/260/A